by William Lawrence
illustrated by Bob Masheris

HOUGHTON MIFFLIN   BOSTON

Printed in China

ISBN-13: 978-0-547-01819-5
ISBN-10: 0-547-01819-3

8 9 10 0940 16 15 14 13
4500408731

I can see a dog.

I can see a rabbit.

I can see a fish.

I can see a bird.

I can see my pet!

Responding

TARGET SKILL **Compare and Contrast** What pets does the boy see in the pet shop? How are they the same? How are they different?

✏️ **Talk About It**

Text to Self Draw a picture of two pets you would like to have. Label the pets. Tell how they are the same and different.

TARGET SKILL **Compare and Contrast** Tell how two things are alike or not.

TARGET STRATEGY **Monitor/Clarify** Find ways to figure out what doesn't make sense.

GENRE **Informational text** gives facts about a topic.